BBQ at the Prom !!

—

A short dramedy for elementary or middle school

by
Jackie Jernigan

www.studentplays.org
info@studentplays.org

<u>Copyright information. Please read!</u>

☞ About Student Plays ☜

Student Plays consists of **John Glass, Jackie Jernigan,** and **Dominic Torres.** We are a group of playwrights and directors that have written scripts for elementary school through college. We are proud of the variety of ages that our scripts serve.

Student Plays has "creepy" plays, and we also carry Latino-themed plays. These are scripts that focus on Latino youths and the Latino experience. Any school can perform a Latino-themed play: it just requires a general introduction and basic exposure to the Spanish language, something that most schools and students already have.

To contact *Student Plays* or to communicate with one of the playwrights, simply email us at info@studentplays.org.

BBQ at the Prom

Characters

LAUREN: Aggressive. Sometimes bossy.

JACKIE: Passive, kind.

JADA: Kind. Jada likes Bobby.

AARON: Aggressive. Sometimes bossy.

BOBBY: Kind. Bobby likes Jada.

DEREK: Nice but outspoken. Tends to follow Aaron's lead.

The setting is an elementary or middle school, somewhere in the United States. The time is the present. It is spring, and the characters are all on a prom/dance committee, and are responsible for planning everything for the end-of-the-year dance.

Any variation of a 'school dance' could be used. A prom, or ball, or just the word 'dance.'

<u>SCENE ONE</u>

As the lights go up, LAUREN, DEREK, AARON, and JACKIE are all seated at a table, looking at various papers and talking about the annual prom. It is springtime, a Monday afternoon, just after school.

LAUREN: You want to serve barbecue at the prom? Who does that?

DEREK: Lots of schools, actually.

LAUREN: Okay, name one.

JACKIE: And what is this gym business? You guys want to have the prom in a *gym*?

AARON: I like the idea. We can decorate the basketball goals, you know, and maybe have baseball jerseys hanging up.

LAUREN: It's a prom, genius, not a sporting event.

DEREK: It might be cool, though! Open your mind up.

(Enter BOBBY and JADA, holding several pieces of paper.)

LAUREN: Whatever. Mrs. Reed would never approve of that.

AARON: How do you know?

BOBBY: Guys, look at all these places we get to pick from!

JACKIE: What is that?

JADA: A list of the restaurants that will cater to the prom.

DEREK: Oh, cool! Let me see!

BOBBY: Look! We can get barbecue! You know how Mr. Cook loves barbecue!

AARON: I know. Remember that one day when he had it in his desk?

DEREK: Yeah!

AARON: His class smelled like chicken and ribs for a whole week!

LAUREN: Uh, barbecue is messy. We can't have that.

DEREK: Why not?

LAUREN: It will be all over the place. That's why.

JACKIE: Yeah.

BOBBY: It's not *that* messy.

JADA: It kind of is.

BOBBY: What do *you* guys want to have? Chicken pasta and ladyfingers?

JACKIE: Yeah, maybe.

AARON: What's a ladyfinger?

JACKIE: *(Pointing to paper.)* Look, here's a place that has pasta.

AARON: We're not doing pasta.

JADA: I like pasta. Bow tie pasta, especially.

LAUREN: Look, guys, we don't have much time!! We have to decide on everything by Friday!

JACKIE: Well, that's what we're trying to do, right?

LAUREN: Yes, but we're never going to agree on the food. Jada, did you bring that music list too?

JADA: Well, I *had* it until Bobby grabbed it.

BOBBY: I didn't grab it.

JADA: Yes you did.

BOBBY: Here. *(Pulls it from his pocket.)* I've got it right here.

JADA: See, I told you.

LAUREN: Okay, let's see . . .

(Pause as they all look at it.)

DEREK: We can do any of these songs?

JADA: Yep.

AARON: Wow. I wanna hear the TrollDaddies.

BOBBY: Cool. I wanna have lots of Townboy.

JACKIE: They're letting us play songs by *these* groups?

DEREK: I like DJ Jonestown. Let's pick him.

JADA: He's dirty.

LAUREN: I know. Why are they letting us play *him*?

AARON: Because he's sick! I love DJ Jonestown.

LAUREN: I know he's *sick.*

AARON: That's not what I mean.

JACKIE: I sort of like the Supremes and the Temptations.

AARON and BOBBY: Who?

DEREK: The Supremes? You like them?

JACKIE: At least they're not dirty.

DEREK: But they're old.

JACKIE: Lots of things are *old*. Basketball is old. So is cheese cake. They've been around for a long time. You don't make fun of *them*, do you?

LAUREN: We might as well decide on the music later because we're not going to agree on anything right now.

DEREK: *You're* not in charge, are you?

LAUREN: No. Why? I didn't think anybody was in charge.

DEREK: Well, you keep making all of the decisions.

LAUREN: I am not. I'm only saying we should wait until later.

BOBBY: *(Suddenly realizing.)* Oh guys, we forgot about the theme!

AARON: Oh, that's right! The theme for the dance!

LAUREN: We have to do that, too?

JACKIE: Yep.

DEREK: How about 'cowboys and indians'? Like in the old days?

JADA, JACKIE and LAUREN: NO!!

DEREK: Awww!

JADA: I was thinking about 'a night under the stars.'

BOBBY: What?

LAUREN: Yeah! Like in Hollywood!

AARON: That's corny.

LAUREN: *You're* corny.

AARON: No, *you* are!

JACKIE: Guys, stop! Look, what about 'an evening with America's legends'?

BOBBY: What??

JACKIE: You know, we could do some historical heroes. People like John Adams, or Florence Nightingale or Thomas Jefferson.

DEREK: We can't hang up posters of a bunch of old dead people in the gym! That would never work!

LAUREN: I told you, we're not going to have the prom in the gym!

BOBBY: Why not?

LAUREN: We can't have it in the gym because Anthony uses a wheelchair, genius. All you guys think about is sports. The gym isn't wheelchair accessible.

DEREK: Anthony? He's not going to the prom!

JACKIE: WHAT?? *(A big pause.)* That is not respectful. You don't know if he's going to the prom or not.

DEREK: Okay, sorry. I didn't mean anything.

AARON: Look . . . this isn't working.

LAUREN: What's not?

BOBBY: We don't agree on anything.

DEREK: Yeah, you guys keep trying to make all the decisions.

LAUREN: We are not!

BOBBY: You kind of are.

DEREK: Yep.

LAUREN: Well, if you guys can do such a better job, why don't you make your own committee?

JACKIE: Lauren!

JADA: No, I like her idea.

AARON: So do I.

JACKIE: You guys can't be serious.

DEREK: If Aaron is, then I am too.

JADA: The same goes for me and Lauren!

BOBBY: Aww, come on, guys.

AARON: The girls can pick the things they want, and the boys will pick the things they want. And we'll see whose selections Mrs. Reed likes.

LAUREN: You're on.

JACKIE: What are we doing here . . ? We're supposed to be working *together*.

JADA: No, let them have their silly ideas! Mrs. Reed will never choose what they come up with!

DEREK: Don't forget, Mr. Cook is involved with the prom too.

BOBBY: Yep, that's true.

DEREK: He'll like what we pick.

AARON: Yeah! And he loves barbecue! I can see him now: "Quiet! I'm enjoying my ribs!"

(The boys laugh.)

JADA: You three are crazy.

AARON: Yeah, well we'll just see about that. Come on, guys.

(They begin to exit.)

DEREK: Not guys, *Boys.*

AARON: Yeah! Boys!

DEREK *(Chanting)***:** Boys, boys, boys . . . we put away our toys!

(The other boys join in as they march out of the room, comically, still chanting. The girls stare in disgust.)

DEREK, BOBBY and AARON: Boys, boys, boys . . . we put away our toys!

(They repeat this as they exit.)

LAUREN: Come on, girls. Let's get out of here!

(They exit as well. End of scene one.)

SCENE TWO

Wednesday afternoon, a few days later. The girls are seated, stage right, holding clipboards and papers, discussing ideas for the dance. The boys are seated stage left, also holding clipboards, and they remain silent, almost in a different reality, until it's their turn to speak. The boys can have their heads down or their backs turned, or anything that won't detract attention from the girls as they speak. (The same goes for when the boys begin to speak; the girls should remain still and silent.)

JADA: Wow. It's only Wednesday and we've already gotten so much work done.

JACKIE: Yep.

LAUREN: That's what happens when you have an all-girl committee and you get down to business.

JACKIE: Silly boys. What do they know?

LAUREN: Yeah! There's a reason why God created girls and the devil created boys. *(To JACKIE)* Even if some of us *do* have silly ideas. Florence Nightingale! Thomas Jefferson! What were you thinking?

JACKIE: Excuse me?? Those were important leaders!

JADA: I still think Mrs. Reed might not like what we're doing. And what about the guys? Has anybody talked to them?

JACKIE: The boys?

JADA: Yeah.

LAUREN: No, and it can stay that way.

JADA: But what is Mrs. Reed going to say now that the committee is different?

LAUREN: She's going to say that she loves our ideas! She's a girl, too!

JACKIE: Yeah!

LAUREN: Come on, let's get to work.

JADA: Alright. So this whole thing is due Friday, right?

JACKIE: Yep.

LAUREN: Two more days. We have plenty of time. Okay, we have the theme, don't we?

JADA: Yes. 'A night in Hollywood.'

JACKIE: With America's legends . . .

LAUREN: We are *not* doing that!

JACKIE: Just kidding.

LAUREN: 'A night in Hollywood' will be perfect. Okay, we've got to decide on the music.

JADA: Oh, here's the song list.

> *(Pause. They look through a book/list of songs)*

JADA: Hmmm. I like these songs right here.

JACKIE: I forgot which ones I picked out.

LAUREN: Jackie, you gave me the songs you want. *(Pointing to paper.)* I have them right here. Jada, you want *these* songs? The ones underlined?

JADA: Yeah.

LAUREN: Okay. Frankie G. Sunset Five. Moxy Rocks.

JADA: Yep.

LAUREN: Those are the same ones that Carolyn and Mandy liked. Actually, me too. So that's settled. What's next?

JACKIE: We've got to get the balloons and the other decorations.

JADA: Right. That should be easy.

LAUREN: Yeah, we can do that tomorrow in study hall. Oh, what about the location for the dance? We talked about having it in the cafeteria, right?

JACKIE: Yep. I like that.

JADA: Sounds fine to me.

LAUREN: Good. The cafeteria it is. What else?

JADA: The food.

LAUREN: Right! Okay, so what were we talking about? What did we want to eat?

JADA: Bow tie pasta and lemon chicken.

LAUREN: Oh, right.

JACKIE: I like the sound of that.

JADA: Yeah, me too. You know how much I like bow tie pasta.

LAUREN: See, *this* is why I like our committee! I like chicken and pasta too!

JADA: So it's settled, then. We agree on the food, right?

JACKIE: Yep.

LAUREN: Fantastic.

JADA: Yeah. That's great.
(Beat. She stands and slowly walks off.)
That's really great.

JACKIE: What's wrong?

JADA: Nothing.

LAUREN: Jada, what is it?

JADA: Nothing. *(Slowly.)* It just seems . . . like we agree on everything.

JACKIE: I know.

LAUREN: Are you sure *that's* what's wrong?

JADA: Huh?

LAUREN: Jada, I think you miss Bobby.

JADA: Stop.

LAUREN: You do. You've been pouting all week! Ever since we formed our own group.

JADA: Whatever.

LAUREN: Think about it, Jada. We're getting so much more work done on our own. We're not arguing.

JACKIE: That's true. And we don't have any ridiculous ideas.

JADA: I know. But . . . .

JACKIE: But what?

JADA: Well, it's like I just said. We agree on almost everything. It's almost boring.

JACKIE: Well, we don't agree on *everything*. Remember the cover of the prom invitations?

LAUREN: Right! You two wanted pink lace and I wanted blue.

JADA: But that was a very minor thing. We still agree on almost everything else.

LAUREN: What about Jackie's silly history ideas?

JACKIE: Exactly! *(To LAUREN)* Wait, *what?*

LAUREN: She wanted to have a Thomas Jefferson or a Ronald Reagan dance, or whatever it's called.

JACKIE: It wasn't going to be called *that*!

JADA: We still quickly agreed, though, didn't we? And . . . it just seems like we usually have the same ideas. I think we need more . . . variety on the committee.

LAUREN: You just miss Bobby, Jada.

JADA: No I do not!

LAUREN: Yes you do. Correct me if I'm wrong—

JADA: I will.

LAUREN: —but you are the one that's always hanging out by his locker.

JADA: Oh please! Bobby's a cheese head.

LAUREN: Well, you must like cheese!

JACKIE: LADIES? *(Pause as they stare at her.)* Can we get to work here?

LAUREN: Sorry.

JADA: Sorry.

JACKIE: Come on. Let's finish this thing.

LAUREN: Alright.

JACKIE: Okay, we have to type all of this up. Here is the format. *(She points to a piece of paper.)* It's got to be neat and organized, just like this.

JADA: I still say we agree on everything, and that it's boring.

LAUREN: I still say you like Bobby. You *Benedict Arnold!*

JADA: Who?

LAUREN: Benedict Arnold.

JADA: Who is that?

LAUREN: I don't know. Some guy a long time ago that betrayed his friends in the army. *(Points at JACKIE)* Ask history girl.

JACKIE: Can we GET TO WORK??? And FINISH THIS??

JADA and LAUREN: Sorry!

> *(They put their heads down, quiet, and the boys instantly come to life.)*

DEREK: It's true! What Aaron was saying is right! Jada's always hanging out by your locker.

BOBBY: Whatever.

AARON: Dude, she actually does.

BOBBY: You two are delirious. Come on, let's get to work.

DEREK: You should win an award for trying to change the subject.

BOBBY: You should win an award for having bad hair.

AARON: Guys, quit! Man! You two should just go put on boxing gloves and go outside! You've been at it all week.

BOBBY: Stop exaggerating. We're only playing.

DEREK: Yeah.

BOBBY: Sort of. Come on, let's finish this prom plan thing. I don't want to miss recess.

AARON: Okay. We agree on the barbecue, right?

DEREK: Right. I can't wait!

AARON: And we agreed on having the dance in the gym, right?

BOBBY: Yep.

DEREK: We also agreed on the athletic jerseys.

BOBBY: I want the Atlanta Braves!

DEREK: I want the Chicago Bulls!

AARON: Relax, we can do both – we don't have to all wear the same thing.

DEREK: Oh, right. And anyway, a bull would eat a brave!

BOBBY: A brave would cut a bull's head off!

DEREK: Please.

AARON: What *is* a brave, anyway?

BOBBY: I don't know. I think it's somebody that—

AARON: Guys, come ON!! We don't have time for that! Now, what else is left?

DEREK: The music.

AARON: Okay. Right. Here's the music sheet, with all of the selections.

(*Pause as they look at it.*)

BOBBY: Hmmm. Guys . . . I don't know about all this.

DEREK: What? What's wrong?

BOBBY: Well, this is going to be a prom, right?

DEREK: Yes. So?

BOBBY: Well, this just seems like one big . . . like one big guys' party. Shouldn't it be . . . kind of fancy, or, maybe classy?

AARON: You sound like them.

BOBBY: Who?

AARON: The girls. You know, the *other* group. Our enemies!

BOBBY: No, I don't. I just think we need more ideas than what we have here.

DEREK: Our ideas are fine.

AARON: Yeah.

BOBBY: What about Mrs. Reed?

DEREK: What about her? We'll turn ours in first and we'll tell her that the girls decided not to be on the committee anymore.

AARON: Yeah.

BOBBY: That's not going to work.

DEREK: You just miss Jada.

BOBBY: What??

DEREK: I think you miss Jada, and that's why you're saying all this.

BOBBY: Uh, *excuse me*? Who is the one that's always hanging out at the girls' table during lunch?

AARON: Guys, we need to finish this!

DEREK: No, *you* are the one that's always hanging out by the girls' table at lunch. You're always over there, talking to Jada.

AARON: GUYS!! Here you go again!!

(Pause. They are stunned.)

DEREK: *(To AARON.)* What, man?

AARON: There's too much testosterone in here, that's what!

BOBBY: Too much what?

AARON: Testosterone. It's when there are too many guys in one place. *(To DEREK.)* Right?

DEREK: Uh, yeah. I think.

BOBBY: Well, we decided to have an all-boy committee. So what did you expect?

AARON: Well, still, can you two just chill??

DEREK: Yeah. Sorry.

BOBBY: Sorry.

AARON: Okay. Back to work. Come on. *(Pointing to the papers.)* We need to decide on the music. We can pick from all these groups and songs, right?

DEREK: Right.

AARON: Okay. Let's see. *(Notices the clock. Beat.)* Oh, wait! Check it out, it's two o' clock. Time for recess!

(They stand, slowly begin to exit.)

DEREK: Yeah, baby!

BOBBY: What about the prom plan?

DEREK: It's not due until Friday. Let's go! Recess!!

BOBBY: Okay.

AARON: Come on, we gotta finish our baseball game. Victor is up to bat, right?

DEREK: Yep, and I'm on deck. Bobby, I want you to pitch today.

BOBBY: Okay. As long as you don't start trying to cause any trouble.

DEREK: And as long as *you* don't start trying to cause trouble.

AARON: Testosterone, testosterone.

DEREK: What does that mean again?

AARON: Oh, be quiet and come on!

BOBBY: Ha!

AARON: I'll tell you what it means later!

> *(They exit in a hurry. The girls must remain still and mute as the boys exit. End of scene.)*

SCENE THREE

Early Friday morning, just before school begins. As the lights go up, LAUREN is waiting for JADA, who enters after a few seconds. They are both carrying their backpacks and their copies of the prom plan.

LAUREN: *There* you are! Hurry up! I want to get this done before the boys get here.

JADA: Okay, okay, I'm here.

LAUREN: You have your copy?

JADA: Right here.

LAUREN: Okay, I've got mine. Where is Jackie?

JADA: She's coming, I guess.

LAUREN: What is she doing? Studying history?

JADA: I don't know. It's seven a.m. I'm sure she's not studying history.

LAUREN: Hmmph. Maybe. With Jackie, you never know. *(Beat.)* Okay, remember: when Mrs. Reed asks us about the boys we'll just say that they let us be in charge of presenting the prom plan.

JADA: Got it. I know.

LAUREN: Jackie just needs to get here so we can go to Mrs. Reed's office and do this.

JADA: Where *is* she?

(Enter the boys. At first, the girls do not see them.)

LAUREN: I don't know! But we have to do this before the boys try it!

AARON: Try what?

LAUREN: Awww! Not you guys!!

DEREK: You girls weren't trying to give Mrs. Reed a copy of the prom plan, were you?

LAUREN: Who? *Us?* Never.

AARON: That's what I thought.

LAUREN: We weren't going to *try* to do it. We were *going* to do it!!

LAUREN and JADA: Ohhhh!

(They high-five each other)

AARON: See, that's the reason that we formed our own group.

BOBBY: And that's the reason that we have the best prom plan in history.

DEREK: Yeah! In *human* history!

JADA: Okay, I just heard the word 'history' two times which is two times too many.

AARON: Yeah? Well, get used to it. History! Get it? *His Story*?? As in, the *boys'* story!

DEREK: Yeah, baby!

> *(They high-five each other. Enter JACKIE, in a hurry.)*

JACKIE: I'm here.

DEREK: Speaking of history, here's the last one of the three stooges.

JADA: Jackie!

JACKIE: Hey.

LAUREN: Where were you?

JACKIE: Sorry! I don't live as close to the school as you guys do!

LAUREN: We could have beaten them to Mrs. Reed if you'd been on time.

AARON: *(Sarcastically.)* She was too busy studying at the library.

JACKIE: No I wasn't!

JADA: At least she wasn't in the *gym*, trying to figure out how we're going to serve *barbecue*!

AARON: Oh, and what did *you* want to serve at the prom? Bow tie pasta?? Ha!

DEREK: *(Sarcastically.)* 'Hi, I'm Jada, and I want pasta.'

AARON: Right, right! 'I'm your waitress, and my name is Jada, and I can bring you pasta'!

DEREK: Ha ha!

BOBBY: Hey, that's enough, guys.

DEREK: What?

BOBBY: That's enough.

AARON: See, I told you he liked her. Bobby Romeo!

DEREK: Ha ha.

JADA: Don't call him that.

LAUREN: Excuse me, Jada??

JADA: What?

LAUREN: Whose side are *you* on? *(To JACKIE.)* See, I knew it! She's a traitor!

BOBBY: Hey!! You be quiet!

LAUREN: No, *you* be quiet!

BOBBY: And if I don't?

LAUREN: We can take it outside if you want to! *(She begins to advance towards the boys, as if to fight.)* Come on, ladies, I'm tired of this!

AARON: Bring it!

LAUREN: Let's go, we can take 'em!

JADA: Lauren what are you doing?

JACKIE: Guys!!

DEREK: *(Joining Aaron, ready to fight.)* Come on!

JADA: HEY!! WAIT A MINUTE!!

(Pause. They stare at her in astonishment.)

LAUREN: What?

JADA: Let's try and chill out, that's what.

BOBBY: Yeah.

AARON: Well, Lauren started it.

BOBBY: It doesn't matter who started it.

JACKIE: This prom thing is getting way out of control.

BOBBY: It sure is. *(Pause.)* And look, Aaron and Derek, there's something I need to say.

DEREK: What is it?

BOBBY: *(Slowly.)* I don't . . .

DEREK: You don't *what*?

BOBBY: I don't want to be in a group that has only boys.

JADA: And I . . .

LAUREN: You don't what?

JADA: I don't want to be in a group that has only girls.

(Pause.)

JACKIE: Um. I kind of agree.

LAUREN: What?? You two can't be serious.

JADA: Yeah, Lauren. I am.

JACKIE: I am too.

LAUREN: We have so much going for us here! We have a cool music list, and—

JACKIE: But that was the *girls'* music list. Not the *group's* list.

LAUREN: But still . . . I like that list!

AARON: And I like *our* list! We have some great songs on there!

JADA: And Aaron, you can still have those songs. You should just . . .

AARON: Just what?

JADA: Well, maybe we could work together, and compromise.

(Pause.)

AARON: Compromise?

LAUREN: Compromise?

JADA: Compromise. You know. Work together?

(Pause. AARON fidgets.)

AARON: But I wanted barbecue!

DEREK: Yeah!

LAUREN: And we wanted bow tie pasta!

BOBBY: Well, can we do both?

JACKIE: Right! Maybe we can do some more research and find a place that delivers both pasta *and* barbecue.

DEREK: Hmmm. Well. That's actually not a bad idea.

AARON: Yes it is!

BOBBY: Aaron, come on, it's actually *not*. I mean, think about it: are we really going to go through life joining boys groups only? How boring would that be?

AARON: Well . . .

BOBBY: We can't always get to have the ideas that we want. You know . . . ?

LAUREN: You guys are all beginning to sound like my grandfather.

JACKIE: Well, Lauren, I've met your grandfather. He usually makes a lot of sense.

LAUREN: True. *(She sighs. Beat.)* Compromise, huh?

JADA: Compromise. Your grandfather will be proud. Your *parents* will be proud.

DEREK: Wow. I can't believe that we're all getting along, for once.

AARON: I know. It's disgusting.

BOBBY: Aaron!!

AARON: I'm only kidding. *(Beat. He begins to exit.)* Well. Let's go, I guess.

LAUREN: Where are we going?

AARON: I guess we need to make a new list before Mrs. Reed gets here.

DEREK: Alright.

LAUREN: Well . . . okay.

JADA: Aaron, a list that includes *all* of us?

AARON: Yes. All of us.

LAUREN: Okay. We can start with the girls music first. And then we'll decide which boys' songs we want to add. And then we'll do the girls—

JACKIE: Uh, Lauren?

LAUREN: Yes?

JACKIE: Um. We're going to compromise, right?

LAUREN: Yeah. I know. Uggh! Compromise!

(They all begin to slowly exit together.)

DEREK: We've got to hurry. Only half an hour before school starts.

AARON: Where we can do this?

LAUREN: Let's go work in the art room. Mrs. Thomas is always here early.

JACKIE: Yeah.

BOBBY: *(Nervously.)* Hey, Jada. Um, are you going to the dance?

JADA: Of course I am.

BOBBY: Oh. Just wondering.

JADA: Oh. Okay.

BOBBY: Yep. Just curious.

AARON and DEREK: *(To BOBBY)* Would you ask her already???

BOBBY: I'm trying to compromise!

JADA: Yes, Bobby. I'll go to the dance with you.

BOBBY: Oh. Okay. Great!!

JADA: I can't wait!

LAUREN: Gosh. This compromising business is going to make me gag.

BOBBY: I know what can cure *that*!

LAUREN: What?

BOBBY: Barbecue!!

LAUREN, JADA and JACKIE: AGGHHHHH!!!!!

(They exit, laughing. Lights fade, end of play)

☞ More from Student Plays ☜

Othello's Just Another Fellow

Dramedy. **Grades 5-7.** 25-35 minutes. 8 actors: 4 males, 3 females, one teacher (or student portraying a teacher) 3 to 5 extras, if needed. ****A Latino-themed play****

A group of students are involved in a school production of *Othello*, but one of them is disturbed about the lack of diversity in the play. He takes certain steps to disrupt the play but in the end is encouraged by the others to try and make a difference in another, more constructive way. A lesson is learned, and the production is saved from disaster!

Pagasqueeny's Pantry

Comedy. **Middle/High School.** 15-20 minutes. 6 actors: 3 females, 2 males. One student (or a teacher) plays the comical role of the elderly Mr. Pagasqueeny.

Three friends sneak into Mr. Pagasqueeny's home to get something that one of them left behind. But in walks Pagasqueeny and they must hide in the pantry! In this comical play, a lesson is learned about honesty and trust, but it takes a heated discussion in the pantry and a subsequent attempt to escape to find this out!

Una Carta de Abuelo

Dramedy. **Middle/High School.** 35-45 minutes. 10 actors: 1 teacher, 5 females, 4 males. (With the option of 4-5 extra actors in two scenes.)   **A Latino-themed play****

Two cousins discover an old letter in their late grandfather's comic collection that they think leads to treasure! The cousins often butt heads, with one believing that he is more "Mexican," the other believing that some people make too much of a fuss about "being Mexican." Thus, they form their *own* groups in search of what Grandpa hid long ago. But what they find is actually worth more than merely silver or gold.

Barbecue at the Prom!

Dramedy. **Grades 5-8.** 25-35 minutes. 6 actors: 3 females, 3 males

It's a classic tale of guys versus girls! It's a prom committee, and everybody is supposed to work together but differences and opinions get in the way, causing the guys and girls to form their groups. For the end-of-the-year prom, one side wants pasta and lace, the other wants sports and barbecue! The two groups square off but eventually work together, demonstrating the importance of cooperation and compromise.

Going to Guatemala

Dramedy. **High School.** 50-60 minutes. 11 actors. 6 males, 5 females.   ****A Latino-themed play****

A Latino student is chosen at the last minute to join a humanitarian group from his school that is headed to Guatemala. But since his Spanish is weak, he faces ridicule and criticism from certain peers. Jealousy and anger trickle throughout the campus as the trip approaches, and the social buzz of the high school becomes even more hectic when the student's trip money is stolen on campus, jeopardizing his trip.

Stravinsky's Kitchen

Comedy. **High School/College.** 12-15 minutes. 3 actors: 3 males (or females).

Two friends secretly enter the home of an employer to obtain a forgotten object but the homeowner abruptly arrives home while they are there. As they hide in the kitchen's pantry and plot their getaway, the two talk and eventually argue, exposing the true colors of one of them. Upon their hasty exit a mistake is made, and one of them capitalizes on this mistake, resulting in his/her fortune.

Forty Whacks

Drama. Spooky. **High School/College.** 25-35 minutes. 3 actors: 2 females, 1 male.

A pair of siblings have inherited the Lizzie Borden Bed and Breakfast in New England. Although the business was run for decades in a quiet, respectable fashion, one of the siblings is over-ambitious, wanting to unearth an alleged piece of buried evidence within the house. This brings about a chilly uneasiness between brother and sister, and perhaps within the house itself.

John Calhoun and a Thief

Drama. **College.** 35-40 minutes. 3 actors: 2 females, 1 male.

Kicked out of a university PhD program, a bitter and dejected female lifts from the library archives original copies of John Calhoun's personal documents. She is counseled and consoled by her roommates, both of whom have had their own troubles. The protagonist's conscience gets to her, as does the mounting advice of her roommates; but as she seeks entry to other universities her luck turns to worse, and the subsequent decisions she makes regarding the papers cause this one-act play to become darker, if not funnier.

Honoring the Hijacker

Drama. **College.** 12-15 minutes. 4 actors: 2 females, 2 males.

It's 1981, the ten-year anniversary of the famed hijacker D.B. Cooper. The play's four characters are attending a "D.B. Festival" and have stayed up very late, outlasting everybody else. The late night chit-chat goes from pranks and jokes to outright volatility, and suddenly this get-together becomes something that three of the four characters didn't bargain for.

It's a Super Day at Sammy's!

Comedy. **Middle or High School.** 35-40 minutes. 9 actors: 5 females, 4 males (4 possible adults).

Jodi has found a summer job at a travel agency. But her three younger siblings can't seem to live without her! They call her at the office incessantly, which interferes with the work. The standard telephone greeting "It's a super day at Sammy's!" becomes a repeated theme of this comedy, as Jodi struggles to reach a balance between her job and her nagging siblings

Three Tenners

Comedy/Drama. **Elementary through High School.** Three Ten-Minute Plays.

Three Creepy Plays

Drama. **Middle School through College.** Three short 'creepy' plays.

Hockey Masks in Hueytown

Drama. Spooky. **High School/College.** 20-25 minutes. 4 actors: 2 males, 2 females.

Driving home for Thanksgiving break, four college students stop off in a small rural town to retrieve one of the student's old family pictures. They reluctantly enter the empty home of his deceased uncle, a former producer for the Friday the 13th movies. Strange objects are found during their search . .   but when a hockey mask surfaces, everything really goes sideways.

The Witch Makes Five

Drama. Spooky. **High School.** 10 minutes. 4 actors: 2 males, 2 females.

After a bizarre group camping trip, a student is checked into a youth mental facility . When she is visited by the other members of the trip, memories of the weekend trickle out . . . and horrific things begin to happen.

Mrs. Calapooza and the Culebra

Dramedy. **Grades 5-8.** 10 minutes. 5 actors: 3 females, 2 males.

Fed up with their grouchy teacher's classroom ways, four students complain and bicker back and forth during a Spanish quiz. The situation grows worse when the friends discover that one of them has pulled the ultimate prank on the teacher.

Raiders of the Lost Rakasa

Dramedy. **Grades 5-8.** 10 minutes. 7 actors: 4 females, 3 males.

Seven young explorers arrive at a cave in a far-off land in search of the great "Rakasa." They find what they want . . . along with a few of the cave's unexpected surprises.

www.ingramcontent.com/pod-product-compliance
Lightning Source LLC
Chambersburg PA
CBHW060542030426
42337CB00021B/4393